# Building a Culture of Collaboration

## How Learning to Manage Conflict Transforms Lives, Organizations and Societies

Michael F. Mascolo, Ph.D.

# DEDICATION

To Becca and Mary

# CONTENTS

# ACKNOWLEDGMENTS

I wish to acknowledge the intellectual contributions of Michael Basseches, Kurt Fischer, Thomas Jordan, Harry Procter, Nicholas Shannon, Iris Stammberger, Jonathan Reams, and David Winter to the ideas contained in this book.

# 1
# WE ARE HAVING DIFFICULTY MANAGING CONFLICT

We're having trouble handling conflict. We are experiencing a crisis of divisiveness at all levels of society. Within *political* spheres, we are deeply polarized[i]. In recent decades, political partisans have increasingly come to view each other as "out of touch", "stupid", "crazy" and even "evil"[ii]. Within *organizations* and *businesses*, conflict between people and among siloed divisions hamper problem-solving and mission effectiveness[iii]; perennial tensions exist among managers and employees over workplace relations. In *schools*, teachers increasingly find themselves having to manage emotional and behavior problems in their students[iv]. *Children* and teens themselves have difficulty managing harassment, bullying, and even violence[v]. In everyday *relationships*, people are struggling to find meaning and connection. The inability to manage conflict is single biggest reason for the failure of marriages and other relationships[vi].

3

There are solutions to these problems. Solving them requires a change in the ways in which we think about ourselves and our relationships with other people. It requires changing the ways in which we think about the nature of conflict itself.

- *Conflict is not a state to be avoided; it is a problem to be solved.*
- *Peace is not the absence of conflict; it is the capacity to resolve it.*
- *If you want to resolve conflict, learn collaborative problem solving.*
- *To solve problems together, connect to the human needs of the other.*

## It's the Relationship, Stupid!

In politics, organizations, and everyday life, managing relationships is the single most important skill that people need. Conflict is inevitable in any relationship. Many people may be surprised to learn that conflict itself is not necessarily a problem. The problem with conflict is how they are *handled*. Managed appropriately, conflict is an opportunity for growth. This can happen when we think of conflict not as a battle between people, but instead as a set of *problems to be solved*[vii].

Most people do not know how to resolve conflict. However, we already know a great deal about how to manage conflict. The problem is that this knowledge is held mainly by professionals – therapists, mediators, counselors and other specialists. However, all people should be equipped with the capacity to resolve social conflict. The ability to resolve interpersonal conflict is not something that is important only in extraordinary circumstances[viii] (e.g., group violence; workplace disputes). It is a skill that is relevant each time we interact with others.

## The Transformative Power of Conflict Resolution

*Learning to resolve interpersonal conflict literally has the capacity to transform lives, relationships, organizations – and even nations.* To realize the transformative power of conflict resolution, it is important to:

(a) *Teach* the principles and practices of conflict resolution to people as early in their development as possible.

(b) Encourage people to adopt *conflict resolution as way of life*. This calls on us to rethink our sense of what it means to be a person and how we relate to others.

(c) Make collaborative problem-solving a foundational practice in *communities, organizations and socio-political life*.

Conflict resolution values transform how we relate to others in our everyday lives. As a result, they can transform ourselves, our relationships, and our communities[ix].

## How We Ordinarily Think of Conflict

A conflict is any form of opposition. When two people get into a conflict or a dispute, there is often some sort of argument. An argument is a kind of competition or contest. Parties to a conflict take sides. Each tries to convince the other that they are right and that the other side is wrong. Arguments are rarely effective. When was the last time that you conceded your position to someone else in an argument? When did you last say, "Yup – you're right and I'm wrong." It doesn't happen very often[x].

An argument is like a game of American football. In a football game, the two teams line up on two different *sides*. They take up their *positions*[xi]. Each team tries to move the football to the opposite side's goal post. As one team moves the ball forward, the other team tries to stop them. When a team moves the ball across the field to the goal post, they score six points. And of course, the team with the most points wins. In a competition, there are winners and losers. The only exception is if there is a tie. In this case, neither team wins nor loses. But both teams can't win at the same time.

Let's use a simple example. Mandy and Mo are planning a vacation together. Mandy wants to the beach while Mo wants to go to the woods. Mandy and Mo can't go to the beach and to the woods at the same time. If they are going to choose one of these options, someone is going to win and someone is going to lose.

What will happen? Mandy and Mo will argue:

Mandy:  I want to go to the beach this year!

Mo:     We went there last year. I hate the sun!

Mandy:  That's not true! We hiked in the sun all day
        yesterday!

Mo:     There's nothing for me to do at the beach.

Mandy:  You always get your way.

Mo:     You mean like you're doing right now?

So, each is trying to convince the other to go to their own preferred vacation spot. Just like a football game, Mandy and Mo are going back and forth. Someone is going to win, and someone is going to lose.

While the winner will be joyous, the loser will be unhappy. The loser will be unhappy because their problem is not solved. They may even feel defeated and humiliated. Such feelings foster emotions like resentment, embarrassment, shame and humiliation[xii]. Resentments fester. And when they do, the losing party will typically be back. When this happens, the conflict will be even worse than before.

There are better ways.

# 2
# WHAT IS COLLABORATIVE PROBLEM-SOLVING?

The trick to solving conflict is to stop thinking it as a battle and start thinking of it as a time for solving problems[xiii]. At first, this seems difficult, because we think of the other party as the problem[xiv]. If the other person is the problem, to solve the problem, we must fight them to get what we want.

But that's not true. The other person is not the problem. The other person is a *person*. They have needs, wants and feelings -- just like you. And just like you, the other person is trying to solve a problem. They are trying to solve the problem of meeting some human *need*[xv].

Let's see how this is done. Let's revisit the problem between Mandy and Mo. In their dispute, Mandy and Mo take different *sides* on the issue of where to go for their vacation. They adopt different *positions*. This is shown in the following:

Go to the
Beach
**POSITION**
Conflict
Go to the
Woods
**POSITION**

Their positions clash: they are in conflict. the couple can't go to the ocean and go to the woods at the same time. So, what do we do?

Let's begin by trying to identify the *problem* that each person is trying to solve. In a conflict, beneath each person's *position* lies a set of deeper human *need*. Needs are a person's deeper desires, wants. We want to understand the underlying *needs* that motivate each person to take the position they do. To do this, we can begin simply by asking "why?"

Imagine that when we ask Mandy why she wants to go to the beach, she says that she wants to be able to *sunbathe and swim*. Imagine that when we ask Mo why he wants to go to the woods, he says that he wants to spend time *camping in nature*.

Now, we have identified the problems that each party is trying to solve. Mandy and Mo have different motives and needs. It looks like this:

Now, what's important to see is that the needs that lie beneath a person's positions motivate those positions! We take the positions we do because they are ways of meeting our needs! In any conflict, *each person is trying to solve the problem of trying to meet their needs.* It looks like this:

Once we have identified each party's underlying needs, the key to resolving conflict is find ways to *meet the needs of both parties* at the same time. The moment we identify the deeper needs and motives of each person in a conflict, we often see that those needs do not necessarily conflict. So, while the positions we adopt in a conflict tend to clash, the needs that motivate them often do not.

This is important. Each party in a conflict is trying to solve a problem – namely the problem of meeting their needs. There are typically many ways to solve any single problem. If this is true, in a conflict, there are many ways to meet each party's needs. The trick is for each party to work together to *find new ways of meeting each other's needs at the same time.*

Instead of pitting one person against the other, collaborative problem-solving pits the two partners against the problem! In collaborative problem–solving, the partners work together to solve the problem of meeting each other's underlying needs.

For Mandy and Mo, one possible solution is for the couple to spend their vacation at a State Park that has a beach near a pond as well as woods for camping and hiking. This way, both partners meet their needs. Problem solved!

### The Big Point: Focus on Needs – Not Positions

*Be kind, for everyone you meet is fighting a hard battle.*

> – Attributed variously to Plato, Philo, Socrates, and others

The most important principle in seeking to resolve conflict is to *focus on needs – never positions*[xvi]. When we enter a conflict, we tend to take different sides. We become locked in our own positions – and we see the other person as opposing us. They are stopping us from getting what we want. We need to stop them! The other party's position is stupid! How can they think like that?

But things change once we see that the other party is probably *not trying to stop us*. Things change when we consider the fact that, just like us, the other person's position is motivated by some unmet need. Just like us, they are trying to solve some problem. Their position is their way of solving it!

Things change once we understand that even though the other person's position may not make sense to us, it does make sense to them![xvii] We often say, "I don't understand how you can think like you do!" But when we do that, we are usually just trying to dismiss the other person. We are saying that they are not thinking clearly, that they are being irrational, or something similar. What would happen we meant it when we said, "I don't *understand* how you can think like that?" What if we said to ourselves, "What you say doesn't make sense to me. But I must assume it makes sense to you. So, let me try to understand how you are thinking and feeling!"

Things change when we realize that, in a dispute, what the other person needs deep down is probably not inconsistent with what we need. If this is so, if we can try to meet each other's needs, we can solve the problem. Once we understand this, we almost immediately become less defensive. We reach out to try to help the other person meet their needs – and the conflict is transformed.

So, let's look at an example. Imagine that Richard and Tanya are both supervisors of Bob. Bob failed to meet a work deadline, and as a result, the firm lost a customer. Tanya wants to Bob to experience consequences of his action; she wants to dock his pay. Richard, however, suggests that they give him a different project.

Tanya is incredulous! She immediately questions Richard's thinking. "Are you crazy? You want to reward Bob for bad work?" Offended, Richard attacks Tanya back, "You are too strict with the employees". How is this situation going to work out? Not well. Both Tanya and Richard are offended. Each sees the other as a problem – as an obstacle to what is wanted.

Things change once we look beneath the positions. What happens if Tanya says to herself, "I don't understand what Richard is thinking! What problem is Richard trying to solve by giving Bob another project? Doesn't he see that that would be rewarding Bob?" So, she asks Richard he would he want to give Bob a new project. Richard says, "I want to give Bob another chance to prove to himself and to us that he can do the work right." Tanya replies, "I have a need to hold Bob to high standards".

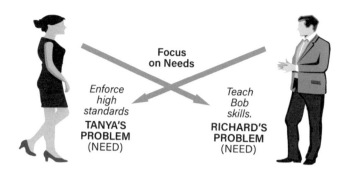

At this point, Tanya and Richard unmet needs – the problems they are trying to solve – come into focus. Tanya sees that Richard is not trying to reward Bob – but in fact wants to help Bob learn to do a better job. Richard learns that Tanya is not trying to be strict, she wants to hold employees to high standards.

At this point, both Tanya and Richard stop seeing each other as the enemy! They stop seeing each other as an obstacle to what each party wants. *Each sees the other's stated position as a reasonable attempt to solve the problem that each is trying to solve.* When this happens, Tanya and Richard can stop seeing each other as opponents and start seeing each other as *partners in a process of problem solving.*

Understanding each other's needs, motives and thoughts, Tanya and Bob can ignore their previously stated positions, and instead work to meet the full range of each other's needs:

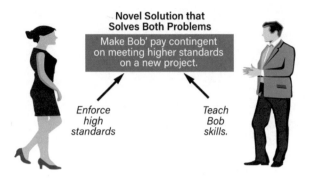

Here we see that there is nothing incompatible about the goal of holding employees to high standards and giving employees a chance to learn needed skills. It is possible to produce novel ways to addresses both motives at once. One such way is to give Bob a second chance and make his pay contingent on his meeting high standards in a new project. Such a solution might motivate Bob more than a punishment, while also teaching him how to be successful.

Again, the success of this approach relies upon the capacity of partners to move beyond what may be their initial reactions to each other – to give each other the "benefit of the doubt" and see that *each party to a dispute is trying to solve a problem that is important to them.* The moment we do this, we experience our incredulity about the other person's position begin to fade. It can begin to become replaced by compassion[xviii], and then genuine shared problem-solving.

## 3
## FOUR STEPS OF COLLABORATIVE PROBLEM SOLVING

There are four basic steps to collaborative problem-solving. These steps are broadly applicable to virtually all forms of conflict – in everyday relationships, in the workplace, in communities, in political life, and even between nations. To be sure, not all conflicts can be solved in this way – but this basic process can be used to solve many more disputes that one might otherwise think possible.

The four steps are:

1. **Connect** to the *humanity* of your partner.
2. **Identify** the genuine *needs* of each party to a conflict.
3. **Brainstorm** *ideas* for meeting the full range of needs of parties to a conflict.
4. **Create** a novel *solution* that meets the needs of all stakeholders to the maximum extent possible.

In the example of the couple planning their vacation,

these steps look like this:

In the initial dispute, the couple adopt different positions on the issue of where to go for a vacation. Mandy wants the beach; Mo wants the woods.

### 1. Connect to the Humanity of the Other

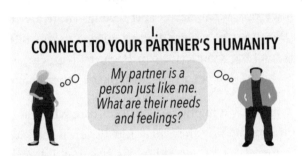

The first step consists of *connecting the other humanity of the other person*[xix]. This step is perhaps the most important – and most difficult! It involves shifting one's attention from oneself and one's own emotions and focusing on the other person. This is often difficult because, in conflict, we are often angry and frustrated. Part of connecting to the other person is calming ourselves. This sometimes requires that we remove ourselves from the conflict long enough to take care of our own negative feelings.

Connecting to the humanity of the other is easy to *say* but difficult to *do*. It means acknowledging the other person's behavior – even their bad behavior – comes from a *human* place. We are always acting to meet our human needs and goals. In a conflict, it is easy to forget that. We tend to think that the other person is intending to hurt us.

Perhaps we think that the other person is acting out of bad intentions. Or we think the other is simply a bad person.

No—connecting the humanity of the other means understanding that the other person is a person, just like us. It means asking, why is my partner taking the position that they do? What needs and feelings motivate them? And the moment we are able to engage in this difficult act, something wonderful can begin to happen: we are able to begin to feel compassion for the other person.

In a conflict, we might say, "I don't care why the other person acts the way they do – I just want what I want!" Or we might say, "Look at how he is acting! I don't want to have compassion! I don't care what they're thinking or feeling."

But that's not good enough. We have to care. We have to care about what the other person wants and needs and how the other person feels. We have to do this for two reasons. First, we have to care about the other person for the sake of the other person. We have to care about the other person simply because the other person is a person worthy of care.

The second reason is that when we care about the other person – when we listen to the other and make them feel heard – they will be more likely to do that for us. Then we can really solve conflicts.

## 2. Identify Each Party's Core Needs

The second step is identifying needs. We can do this in many ways. The most obvious way is to ask the person why they take the position that they do in a dispute. What problem are you trying to solve? What is it that you really need or want? The moment we ask this question, things begin to change.

At the beginning of a conflict, two parties are *against each other*. They are typically on the attack! They are afraid that they are not going to get what they want. And they are probably more afraid that they may lose the argument. Losing an argument causes feelings of embarrassment, shame and even humiliation.

But when we begin to inquire about the needs and feelings of the other, something happens. The other person is surprised! What is this odd thing that my opponent is doing? Do they really care about what I want? And the more one partner seeks to understand the needs, feelings and thought of the other, the safer the other person feels. They begin to realize they may not have anything to fear from their "opponent". Your empathy will cause them to begin to lower their defenses. And when they begin to express their real needs and feelings, your empathy will begin to generate trust.

In the case of Mandy and Mo, we find that what Mandy wants is to sun and swim. What Mo wants is to camp in nature. These are their genuine motives! Are these bad things? Do Mandy and Mo have bad intentions toward each other? No. They have human feelings, human needs and human wants. Time to take care of them.

### 3. Brainstorm Ideas

Once each party's needs are on the table, it's time to start to try to find ways to meet those needs. The goal here is not simply to meet one's own needs – it is to meet the needs of all parties to a conflict. This is why the process is called collaborative problem-solving. All parties to a conflict work together to solve the problem at hand – where the problem is meeting the needs of all constituencies to the greatest degree possible.

You might think that this is the hard part of the process.

Depending on the nature of the problem at hand – the number and complexity of the needs of the people involved – it may or may not be difficult. But, most often, once the needs are expressed, problems all but solve themselves. Once we stop pitting one person against the other, we free ourselves from the burden of having to fight each other. Now, we can begin to think. The hard part is largely over – that is, the emotional task of connecting to both the other's and our own human needs and feelings.

At this step, when we brainstorm ideas, it's important to do so without a lot of judgment or evaluation. Just brainstorm. Generate and list all kinds of solutions to the problem. Generate good solutions, bad solutions, crazy solutions and even ugly solutions. Why? Because the more ideas we generate, the more likely it is that we'll cover all the bases and create a good solution. And also, it's because those bad, crazy and even ugly ideas – the ones that we are afraid to speak about -- often turn out to be the good ones.

So, Mandy and Mo should entertain a lot of ideas before they try to actually solve their problem. They could go to either a beach or the woods. They could go to the beach during the day and the woods at night. They could find a pond near the *woods*. They could find a beach near the woods (huh?). None of these ideas really work, right? However, these bad ideas could lead to a good idea.

## 4. Create a Novel Solution

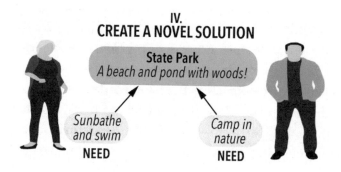

To create means to invent or construct something that *was not there before*. And something is novel if it is new — that is, if it *was not there before*. Most often, the best solutions to a conflict are the ones that *were not there before*.

The best solutions tend to be *new, novel, created, invented*. They are the solutions that *no one could have thought of* before the process of working together! Why is this? Because each party needs to know the needs of the other to create a solution! It can't be done alone! If we only focus on our own "side" of the problem, we will only produce a partial solution. So, we must know the full range of needs that define the problem!

And we need the benefit of each other's intelligence in finding ways to meet the full range of our needs. The other always has a different view than we do. They see things in a different way. And they are going to be able to generate ideas for solving problems that we don't and can't see. We need each other to create truly novel ideas to solve problems. We influence each other; we stimulate each other; we work off each other.

And so, in the end, together, we can create novel solutions that we might not otherwise be able to entertain by ourselves. As Mandy and Mo were working together, let's imagine that one of the "bad" ideas that they created together was going to a "beach by the woods". This idea makes no sense; beaches are not near the woods! Or are they? Many state parks located in the woods have ponds with sandy beaches. Problem solved!

## 4
## AN ETHOS FOR A MORE COLLABORATIVE SOCIETY

When we enter a conflict, we are immediately confronting with some obstacle. Our natural response is to focus on that obstacle and seek to remove it. Most often, we see the *other person* as the obstacle to be overcome. As a result, we prepare for a battle.

As we have seen above, perhaps the most difficult obstacle to overcome in resolving conflict is to see that the other person is *not* the obstacle. The other person is a person, with her own needs, desires, feelings and concerns. As a person, the other has dignity. To the extent that the other person acts out of an attempt to meet their own unmet needs, they deserve our compassion.

And this leads us to what seems to be a contradiction. In a dispute, how can I advance my own needs while simultaneously extending compassion for the other person? Isn't that unnatural? Scholars, philosophers, psychologists and religious thinkers have long suggested that humans are motivated by two broad categories of motives: *fear for the self* and *love for the other*[xx]. This distinction is shown as follows:

*Two Basic Human Motives*

It is often said that humans are primarily self-interested or selfish creatures[xxi]. To be sure, self-interest is an indisputable aspect of the human condition. People act to meet their needs. We are self-interested beings. However, we are not *just* self-interested beings. Humans are also deeply concerned about the well-being of others[xxii]. We act not only out of self-interest, but also out of love, care and compassion for others. Although we act out of both motives, we are not always able to do so *at same time*. Our capacity to act *simultaneously* out of self-interest and compassion for others develops over time.

## Reconciling Self Interest and Care for Others

The capacity to act simultaneously out of self-interest and care for others – when it happens -- is a hard-won developmental achievement[xxiii]. The figure below shows how this happens over time a child's development.

When infants enter the world, they show both an orientation toward both *self-gratification* and *concern for others*. We are all familiar with the self-focused needs of infants. Infants the world with needs that they cannot meet on their own. But even infants are not entirely motivated by self-interest. Concern for others develops gradually over the first two years of life –and becomes increasingly prominent during the second year[xxiv]. Young infants who hear the cries of other infants often themselves begin to cry. Some have suggested that such cries are the early roots of empathy[xxv]. As infants get older, they become increasingly responsive to the pain of others[xxvi]. Their facial expressions of joy shift when a caregiver exhibits signs of pain. Infants in their first year are capable of primitive acts of helping. By 8-9 months, some sometimes help others by fetching objects out of the other's reach[xxvii]. Thus, both self-interest and concern for others are part of what it means to be human from an early age.

Both self-interest and the to care for and assist others develop dramatically over the early years of life. While infants and young children can experience both self-interest and empathic concern for others, they are not capable of experiencing these emotional dispositions *at the same time*. Instead, as shown in the above figure, each of these dispositions and ways of being in the world develop separately – in parallel -- over the first years.

*Reconciling Self-Interest and Care in Development*

Over time, these two lines of development – self-interest and care for others – will inevitably come into conflict. We see this in children every day. Two children are together playing in the yard. There is only one swing. One child takes the swing for herself. Wanting the swing for himself, her friend asks to swing first – and begins to cry when his request is denied. In this situation, the first child is aware of both her own interests (e.g., I want to swing) and those of her friend (e.g., he wants the swing). However, the child's self-interest and concern for his friends are in conflict – and the child does not know how to resolve the conflict. A child may cling to the swing and ignore her friend's pleas, or he may resentfully give up the swing. Perhaps the two children will fight over the swing.

This type of conflict occurs thousands of times over the

course of a child's development. By the time children reach adolescence, they will have developed a great deal of knowledge and skill about how to advance their own interests and how to tend to others[xxviii]. By adolescence and early adulthood, people are capable of much more developed modes of thinking and feeling. They can now face the conflict between self-interest and care for others head on.

When this happens, adolescents find themselves at a choice point. There are at least three ways to resolve the conflict between self-interest and care for others.

1.  I can separate myself from the interests and feelings of others and develop my primary identity around the goal of *self-interest*.
2.  I can push away my own needs and feelings and develop my primary identity around the goal of *serving others*.
3.  I can *reconcile* my conflicting experiences of self-interest and concern for others.

The first strategy is to put myself before others. The second strategy is to put others before me. The third strategy brings these seemingly contradictory feelings together. When this happens, the adolescent (or adult) can begin to *reconcile self-interest with concern for others*. That is, I make your interests, feelings and well-being *part of my own self-interest*. In so doing, I do not lose myself or give myself over to the other – I am aware of my self-interest. Instead, I act out of love and compassion. As I do, I am enhanced by the ways I give *of* myself to you.

## The Need for Self-Transformation

When we experience conflict with others, the first thing we think of is how our interests have been thwarted. In a conflict, we are *suffering*. When this happens, it is natural to put our own unmet needs before our concern for the other person.

However, the other person is also suffering! Compassion calls on us to act out of concern for the suffering of the other[xxix]. And so, if we want to transform conflict into collaboration, we must put our own needs "on hold" long enough to stop ourselves from immediately attacking the other. We need to be able to "check our needs" long enough so that we can consider how the other person's unmet needs – their suffering – leads them to act in the ways that they do.

When I make your needs and interests part of my self-interest, I make *compassion for you* part of *who I am* as a person[xxx]. When this happens, self-interest and care for the other need not be contradictory motives. In fact, I am *enhanced* when I contribute to your well-being. This is like what Eric Fromm says when he speaks of acting out of *love*[xxxi]. If we really love someone, we respect, care and concern for the other. We give *of ourselves* to that person. However, to give *of ourselves* is not a form of self-sacrifice. It is a form of self-enhancement. When I give of myself out of care, I am not diminished; I feel my own power.

In a conflict, the capacity to reconcile my self-interest and my compassion for you allows me to rise above anger and hostility. It allows me to see that I gain nothing by attacking you and denying the legitimacy of your needs. It allows me to see that my request that you meet my needs is tied up with your request that I meet yours.

How we view ourselves and our relationship to each other is central to how we approach conflict[xxxii]. If we want to foster a more collaborative society, we need to foster more collaborative and relational selves[xxxiii].

## This Isn't Kumbaya: We Need both Care *and* Power

The biggest obstacle to conflict management – especially in difficult situations – is the belief that it is simply impossible. People often imagine the process of resolving conflict to be one in which people sit around a circle and are nice to one another. People often think that managing conflict means being nice or giving in to the other party to eliminate conflict. They tend to imagine conflict resolution as, well…the *absence of conflict*! That's not resolving conflict – that's appeasement. Conflict resolution is not *kumbaya*.

Here are some things that conflict resolution – at least as discussed here – is *not*:

- Resolving conflict does not mean *giving in* to the other side.
- Resolving conflict does not mean being *nice* so the other party will do what you want.
- Resolving conflict does not mean *seeking a compromise*.

- Resolving conflict does not mean trying to reason with the other person.

- Resolving conflict does not mean trying to *convince* the other to see things your way.

- Resolving conflict does not mean trying to *persuade* the other party to do something *they don't want to do.*

If people are trying resolve conflict, that means that there is…conflict. You can't resolve conflict by pretending that it is not there, wishing it away, or pleading with the other person. You don't resolve conflict by *giving in* to the other side.

Managing conflict, as discussed here, involves coordinating *needs* between people. It is based on the idea that often (but not aways) it is possible to create ways in which both parties in a conflict can meet their needs. If this is true, then, in a dispute, the only thing I have to convince you of is that *I want to help you meet your needs.*

However, meeting your needs doesn't mean that I am willing to give up meeting my needs. I am not. My needs are inviolate. I'm standing by them. *I am not going to let the other party hurt me.* I am not going to allow the other party to violate my needs. I must assert my own needs as I seek to show you that I am also willing to try to meet yours. The process is a mutual one.

And so, I have two motives in any interaction that I have: I want to meet my needs, and I want to connect to you and meet your needs. In seeking to meet my needs, I will not allow the other to violate them. This means I need both *power* and *compassion*. I need compassion to understand you well enough to be able to connect to your needs. But I need power – the capacity to assert myself – to ensure that I am not hurt and that my needs will be met.

POWER        COMPASSION

### *Open Strength*

This is expressed in the above diagram. In each interaction, I metaphorically hold up two hands. I hold one hand out in a gesture of protection. If the other attacks me or is a threat to me, this hand says, "Stop. I won't allow you to harm me". The other hand, however, is held out, open to the other person. It says, "I am open. What are your needs? How can I help resolve them?"

If needed, the two hands can help each other. Without animosity, I can extend my open hand and say, "I want to help", but extending my protecting hand, I can say, "but I cannot help if you are attacking me. Stop attacking

me, and we can find a way to meet our needs together."
In this way, I use my *protecting hand in the service of my open hand*.

But it also goes the other way around. I see that the other is attacking me. Holding out my open hand – acting empathy and compassion in the face of the other's attack – often has the effect of disarming the other person. When the other sees not only that you are not against them, but that you are willing to help, their anger aggression often dissipates. They are more willing to collaborate. In this case, *the open hand acts in the service of the protecting hand*.

Managing conflict involves acknowledging conflict. We can't acknowledge conflict without asserting our inviolate needs – and holding to them. This is not always pleasant – at least at first. We should not expect conflict resolution to be the absence of conflict. It is not. It is the managing and resolution of conflict.

## What Would It Be Like If We Were Continuously Sensitive to Each Other's Needs?

### Or...

## Why Do You Blow Your Horn in Traffic?

Consider the following common situation. People are driving on a busy street. One driver moves into the other's lane without signaling. The first driver lays on his horn. A finger is raised.

What happened in this situation? What was the first driver communicating with his horn and his finger? "What do you think you're doing? You are violating *my* space! Stay in your lane!"

The streets of Delhi in India are more congested than virtually any other streets in the world. On any given day, cars share the street with trucks, motorcycles (sometimes with entire families riding on a single motorcycle), scooters, bicycles, rickshaws, auto-rickshaws, cows, beasts of burden, and pedestrians. At any given moment, one can hear the constant "beep beep beep" of horns. What is being communicated by those horns?

You can be forgiven if you think the horns mean "You're too close!" or "Get out of my way!" But they don't mean that at all. Instead, they mean, "I'm coming! I'm here! Look out for me!" In fact, it is common to see vehicles exhibiting signs that ask drivers to use their horns:

*Photo by Angela Carson, 2024*

What's the difference?

The American and Indian approach to beeping the horn

in traffic is shown in the diagram that appears below. As shown in the left panel, in the United States, we see ourselves as separate and distinct individuals. I have the right to pursue my own agenda as what I do does not violate your right to do the same. I can't violate your boundaries, and you can't violate mine. If you do, we have a conflict.

In traffic, this literally occurs! We have explicit rules that indicate when we must "stay in our lanes". One person has the "right of way" and the other does not. If you cross the line, I'll beep my horn to tell you are violating my space. I'll also beep to tell you that you are driving too slowly. The system of boundaries and rules is a very efficient way of organizing traffic (and social interaction in general).

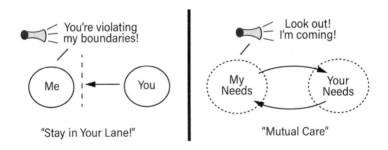

### Honking to Separate versus Honking to Connect

Now, this efficient system for regulating traffic (that is, for regulating social relations on the streets) comes at a price: *road rage*. In "road rage", you've violated my *boundaries* – my *rights*. When my rights are violated, I become angry to defend myself against your intrusion on my space. You have not only violated my space, but you have violated *me*. I lash out in rage to defend my honor.

The Indian approach, shown on the right side of the figure, is different. Indian traffic is congested, confusing, and convoluted. To deal with the chaos, there is a shared ethos of "looking out for one another" or "warning you that I'm coming". Honking the horn is not typically experienced as an aggressive act. In fact, it is encouraged so that I can let you know that I'm here. I beep so you can adjust to me while I attempt to adjust to you.

We can use the rules of traffic in the US and India as metaphors for how we think of ourselves and our relationships to each other. The United States is an individualistic nation. We see ourselves as separate and distinct from one another. We value the *rights* of the individual person. Each person has rights – but "my rights end where your nose begins". As a result, each person is expected to stay more-or-less "in their own lane."

The "look out for each other" approach is different. In this approach, we don't see ourselves as separate and independent individuals with fixed or rigid boundaries to defend. Instead, we see each other as connected. We have duties and responsibilities to each other. Instead of simply acting to make sure that we respect each other's rights and boundaries, we act out of a sense of *care* for each other. I look out for you, and you look out for me.

## 5
# EXAMPLES OF COLLABORATIVE PROBLEM SOLVIING IN ACTION

Collaborative Problem-Solving is an interpersonal process. It takes place between at least two people. However, its effectiveness extends far beyond everyday relationships. This chapter contains examples of the use of conflict management in three different settings: a business situation, in a relationship between friends, and in a political context. The first two are descriptions of actual events. The last is an example of how conflict resolution principles can be used to bridge political divides on a contentious social issue, namely the question of gun violence.

## I.
## This is a Business -- Not a Charity!

A student in our undergraduate conflict resolution course asked about why conflict resolution principles should be applied to business. He said, "The company I work for buys and sells buildings. We bought a building in a residential area, honoring all the legal requirements. Now the neighborhood doesn't want us to rebuild. They want to maintain the historical feel of the neighborhood." In a critique of what I was teaching, he asked, "Why should we want to honor their 'needs'? After all, we are a *business* – not a *charity*."

We talked about how, beyond having compassion for people who live in the neighborhood, it may be good business to seek to have happy neighbors. We left it at that. Several months later, the student spontaneously announced to the class that he said that he had told his boss about the process of negotiating conflict to create "win-win solutions". The boss was apparently curious about the concept. The business was scheduled to raise the old home that they had purchased and replace it with new and modern building in its stead. The neighbors objected to new plan for house. The boss and his team decided to meet with the neighbors. They sought to identify what type of building they would find acceptable in the space. The neighborhood indicated their desire to have the building remain, but to have it refurbished in some way.

This solution was not feasible for economic and municipal (zoning) reasons. However, the boss and his team sought to find a solution that would meet a triad of needs: the economic needs of the business, the aesthetic needs of the neighborhood, and the zoning needs of the local municipality. They developed a proposal that would involve building a new structure from the ground up –

but one that would resemble the old structure. The proposal proved agreeable to the neighborhood. It also turned out that when the boss brought the matter to the local zoning board, they also not only approved it, but the new structure created conditions that allowed the business to purchase additional lands to improve the property further.

An idea that developed between a professor and a student in an undergraduate class blossomed into a proposal that produced a win-win-win outcome that affected real people in a real community. While we could say that this collaboration occurred in a *business* context, it spanned multiple spheres of interpersonal activity. It operated as an interpersonal process that occurred between many groups of people – between the professor and the student; the student and the boss; the boss and his staff; the staff and the neighborhood; the people within the neighborhood itself; and between the boss and the zoning board. The process spanned interpersonal, business and political contexts.

## II.
### "That's Retarded!":
### A Collaborative Alternative to Cancel Culture

It is currently common for people in some social groups to seek restrict the use of words that can be regard as offensive to some social groups. One such term is "retarded". Often, when such terms are used, people feel obligated to confront the offender to express their discomfort. In some circumstances, the use of certain terms can be seen as a sign of bias, bigotry, or prejudice that results in the offending party being "canceled" – that is, shamed or shunned from participation the activities of the offended group.

The following account contains a description of a situation involving two friends – Chris and Jake. Chris was uncomfortable with Jake's use the term "retarded" as a pejorative. In the account that follows, assisted by a mediator, Chris was able to have a conflict resolving discussion with Jake about the use of the term "retarded". Unlike many discussions about such issues, this conversation was able to occur without Jake feeling demeaned or being cancelled. *More important, both partners were transformed by the discussion.* Surprisingly, as a result of their capacity to listen carefully to the needs, feelings and perspectives of the other, *both partners transformed their perspective on the issue at hand* – namely, the use of the term "retarded". This discussion shows how collaborative problem-solving provides an alternative to adversarial ways of addressing social problems.

Chris started the discussion. The mediator urged Chris to state his concerns by expressing the needs and feelings that emerged when Jake's used of the term "retarded":

Chris: When those kind of terms are used, I feel disrespected, and I feel like there is a lack of empathy for different groups of people because as just someone who is a member of that community and who has relatives to are mentally disabled and handicapped, I have a need for people to be respectful to those groups of people, to myself, to people of my family and who are also disabled..

Jake was able to summarize Chris's concerns in a non-judgmental way that made Chris feel both heard and understood. The mediator modeled the process of seeking to understand – in an empathic and nonjudgmental way – why Jake used the term "retarded" in everyday conversation:

Jake: When I use those terms... Well, I feel like maybe my need when using that *describes* something is part ...just...a way to look ...that's...I use that as in my mind it's a descriptor and also use it I maybe to be *humorous* in some way...*I want people to like me* and by being funny is one way that I can do that and that is a way that previously allowed me to be humorous with other people.

Here we see that Jake uses the term in ways that were successful in gaining the affection of previous friend group. Even though Chris does not like the use of the term "retarded", he was able to understand why Jake may use the term in order to be liked by his peer. The mediator attempted to further understand what it was like for Jake to use the term "retarded":

Mod: These are words that people in your group used, how do you feel when they use those words? Do you feel that they are funny words? ... Do you ever have bad feelings or do you have good feelings about them?

Jake:    I feel differently [in different contexts]. If they are ever directed at someone directly, meaning for the purpose of … When it's used jokingly, which is like I guess subjective, but when I perceive it as jokingly, I find it funny.

Mod:     So you are saying that if you see someone use words like "gay" or "retarded" directed at someone else…

Jake:    …in a harmful way…

Mod:     In a harmful way that make you feel uncomfortable

Jake:    It makes me feel disgusted.

Clearly, Jake has a more nuanced understanding of the use of the term "retarded" than Chris had thought – or even as Jake had previously thought. Sensing that there was more that Jake wanted to communicate, the moderator probed Jake's experience further.

Mod:     [Is there anything else that] you want Chris to know that you feel that he doesn't know?"

Jake:    Okay. I also use the word "retarded" to describe myself sometimes. not severe., but I have mental stuff sometimes, kind of…I feel like it applies to me in some way…. Even not to the extent…I don't know.

Mod:     Great, good. That's good., And why is it important to you that he knows that?

Jake:   Because I feel that I also…the word is kind of a
        part of me? I don't know. Sometimes..I don't
        know…

At this point, Jake has revealed something truly
remarkable and unexpected. He *identifies* – at least in part
– with the term "retarded". This is something that neither
Chris nor the Moderator could have anticipated before
the conversation – and something that would have been
almost impossible to learn outside of a problem-solving
conversation in which Jake was made to feel safe and
accepted. This realization will ultimately transform
Chris's understanding of the issue.

Chris is now really beginning to understand Jake.
Stumbling over his own words, Chris wants to express
the fact of his understanding:

Chris:  So, you feel because you identify with the
        community of people that maybe like mentally
        disabled at least on some level, and you find that
        you resonate with that word, either in a joking
        sense or not in a joking sense, so that is why you
        use that word …

Mod:    What is it like for you to identify with a word that
        some people see as a negative? What is that like
        for you?

Jake:   I guess I also see it as a negative. I feel that
        sometimes I am "less than" because of things.

Chris:  So you feel like…because you do certain things

43

and act in certain ways that you resonate with the word "retarded" because sometimes you feel lesser...

Jake:   Yeah.

Guided by the moderator, Chris and Jake were able to create an agreement of how to proceed with the issue of Jack's language. No – Chris did not change his feelings that the term "retarded" should be avoided. But he did understand Jake's use of the term and felt much more tolerant about the term. He came to understand that not all uses of seemingly bigoted or stereotypical terms could be understood in that light. Jake came to understand how others felt about the use of the term, and spontaneously volunteer to limit or even eliminate the use of the term from his vocabulary.

Here we have a shared solution to a problem that could have easily degenerated into a confrontation involving shameful accusations of ignorance, bigotry, or worse. Chris could have easily positioned himself as morally superior to Jake (indeed, he actually did at the beginning of the discussion), calling on Jake to renounce his use of an offending term. By compassionately seeking mutual understanding of each other's needs, feelings and beliefs the conflict all but resolved itself. This example shows the importance of moral humility, genuine curiosity and compassion in the process of resolving sensitive social problems.

## III.

## Bridging Political Divides:
## The Example of Gun Violence

In the United States, people differ in their views about whether to restrict the availability of guns to citizens. At its most basic, the question under debate is:

*Should we permit or regulate gun ownership?*

For some, the issue is addressed by the First Amendment to the *United States Constitution*, which states: "A well regulated Militia, being necessary to the security of a free State, the right of the people to keep and bear Arms, shall not be infringed". Many argue that gun ownership is a right protected by the Second Amendment. Citizens in favor of gun control argue that government has both the right and responsibility to ensure the public good. Part of this responsibility is protecting the public from the dangers of firearms. Advocates of gun regulation and gun rights tend to engage in heated debates over the extent to which the Second Amendment guarantees the right of citizens to own guns.

As long as the issue is organized around this sort of debate, it is unlikely that there will be meaningful or lasting solutions to the problem of gun violence. The gun debate, as traditionally framed, requires people to make a zero-sum choice: either we permit or restrict guns? The goal of permitting guns is in direct conflict with the goal of restricting them. It is not surprising that such a stark choice would quickly divide the room:

| Gun Rights | CLASHING POSITIONS | Gun Control |
|:---:|:---:|:---:|

### *Clashing Political Positions*

But this question is not framed as an attempt to *solve a problem*. Indeed, the genuine problem is never actually stated in the question. The problem at hand is not whether to permit or restrict guns. In fact, gun regulation is proposed as a *solution* to a problem – namely, the problems of *how to reduce gun violence*. Similarly, advocating the permitting of gun ownership is not a kind of problem. It too is a *solution* to a problem – namely that of *ensuring that people can use guns for their chosen purposes*.

When the issue is stated in this way, there is no alternative to thinking of the conflict as a type of battle. Each side tries to advance their position at the expense of the other. This is what typically occurs in political debates and campaigns. Political debates are not about solving problems; they are about advancing positions.

In collaborative problem-solving, the battle over positions is turned into a kind of problem-solving. That is, instead of battling over whether nor not to permit guns, the parties seek ways to solve the full range of problems that motivate the conflict in the first place:

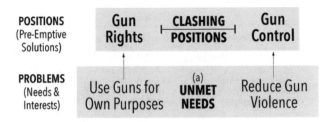

***Look to the Unmet Needs***

When this happens, the process starts not with, should we permit or restrict guns, but instead the statement of a problem to be solved -- something like:

*How can we simultaneously reduce gun violence while simultaneously honoring the desire of people to own guns?*

Collaborative problem-solving begins by articulating *problems*. The most important part of problem-solving is representing the problem itself. There are typically *multiple diverse solutions for any given problem*. If this is so, then once each party is assured that the "other side" is willing to acknowledge, respect and even try to help solve each other's problems, fears begin to subside. Parties can then begin working together – without fear – to find new ways to simultaneously solve each other's problems. When this happens, novel solutions tend to emerge – often, with minimal effort.

So, how can we reduce gun violence while simultaneously protecting gun ownership? If we are open to novel ways of thinking, we can see that there are many possible ways that these problems can be solved simultaneously. These are shown here:

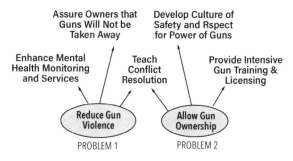

## *Bridging Political Divides on the Issue of Gun Violence*

In the case of gun violence, the moment we look beyond entrenched political positions, we can find that there are many ways to meet each side's underlying needs and interests. Much gun violence occurs because of problems associated with lack of education, economic need, poverty and the poor means of resolving conflict. If this is so, then core origins of gun violence can be addressed by improving the infrastructure of communities, such as fostering educational attainment and economic mobility.

A national effort to teach effective conflict resolution help provide people with skills to solve social problems before then rise to the level of lethal conflict. Still further, most acts of gun violence occur because of suicide. Direct interventions to address the circumstances under which people choose to take their own lives (e.g., hopelessness, collapse of meaning, feeling left behind, depression) can help address the root causes of suicidality.

A major problem with the debate on gun violence is that gun owners — the vast majority of whom have deep respect for firearms — fear that political figures are motivated to take their guns away. Understanding the needs of gun owners can bring awareness to this issue. To the extent that their desire to use gun responsibly will not be thwarted, gun owners may be more likely to join forces with those who are concerned about gun violence to identify novel solutions to difficult problems. Given such assurances, it is likely that many gun owners would applaud the desire to promote a culture of responsible gun ownership, complete with rigorous training programs and even licensure for gun ownership.

People will rarely if ever attain full agreement on ways to solve collective problems. To be sure, in the solution described above, the full range of issues related to gun violence would not be resolved. However, collaborative solutions like that described above would nonetheless go a long way toward *reducing the number gun deaths in society while simultaneously ensuring freedom of gun ownership.* Collaborative solutions hold out the promise of meeting many of the needs of diverse parties to a conflict.

# 6
# STRATEGIES FOR COLLABORATIVE
# PROBLEM-SOLVING

The process of collaborative problem-solving begins before you engage attempt to resolve any given conflict. Collaborative problem-solving goes more smoothly if you can develop a *Collaborative Mindset.* The Collaborative Mindset is the idea that solving problems with others requires the development of a compassionate understanding how and why others do what they do.

At its most basic, the Collaborative Mindset consists of an appreciation of two principles: *compassion* and *credulity.* *Compassion* means acting out of concern for the *suffering* of the other person. *Credulity* is the idea that even though what the other person thinks, feels, says, or does may not make sense to us, *it makes sense to them*. Internalizing and acting on these principles can transform how you relate to others and the quality of all of your relationships.

Let's start with *credulity*. In a conflict, we disagree with the other person. As a result, we may feel that we don't understand why the other person acts as they do. We may think that their thinking is inferior, that they are ignorant, stupid or even crazy. The problem is that the moment we think of someone this way, we give up the possibility of solving a problem with them. We've already dismissed them. This is the worst thing we can do.

As stated throughout, we are always acting to meet our unmet needs, goals, and concerns. If this is true, no matter how crazy we think the other person may be, the other person has reasons for acting the way they do. Don't assume that their needs, feelings, and values are the same as yours! People differ dramatically in how they understand and interpret the world. If you want to play a role in solving a problem with someone – if you want to resolve conflict – you are going to have to try to understand, in a deep way, what needs they are trying to meet.

And so, the first part of the Collaborative Mindset is to see that the other person is a person – just like you. They are doing "the best they can" with the knowledge, experiences and resources available to them. To understand the other person, try to identify their needs, feelings and beliefs. *It doesn't matter if, at first, they don't make sense to you. Keep asking questions to find out how the other person's beliefs, needs, feelings and actions make sense to them.*

Once this happens, you will understand that the other person is fighting a great battle. They are trying to solve a problem – to meet some unmet need. And if this is happening, at some level, your partner is suffering. And your partner is not the only one suffering: you are too. Once you can understand the other person's behavior as an attempt to fulfill some human need, you feel likely feel compassion for them (even if you were or are still frustrated or angry with them). And the more you see that you are trying to fulfill an unmet need, you can begin the process of feeling compassion for yourself.

Ultimately, a Collaborative Mindset develops slowly through practice – by engaging others repeatedly in collaborative problem-solving whenever a conflict, however grand or trivial, arises. Let's look at some strategies for engaging in each of the four steps of collaborative problem-solving.

## Strategies for Collaboration

Let's go through each of the four steps of collaborative problem-solving. Here are some ways you can connect with your partner and solve problems together.

## 1. How to Connect to the Humanity of the Other

Connecting to the humanity of the other is the first step to collaborative problem solving, but it is not restricted to the first step. It must occur throughout the entire process. Here are some ways, however, to start off the process.

***Adopt the Collaborative Mindset.*** The best way to connect to the humanity of the other is start with a Collaborative Mindset. In a dispute, if you start with a disposition of compassion and credulity, you will always be saying to yourself, "I don't like what this person is saying (thinking, feeling or doing). Why are they doing saying this? What problem are they trying to solve? What unmet need are they trying to fill?" The moment you do this, you start to transform the interaction.

***Calm down.*** You can't solve problems when you are angry. And I repeat: you can't solve problems when you are angry. It doesn't happen. If you are angry, calm down. If you can't calm down, say something like, "I am too angry right now to engage in a constructive conversation. I'm going to go away and take care of my anger. When I have, I'll come back, and we can talk." You also can't solve problems when your partner is angry. If your partner is angry, try to use empathy to calm them down. If that fails, and your partner remains angry, you can say, "I see that you are angry. I can't have a conversation with you when you are angry. Let's postpone this until we are both calm." If that fails, simply remove yourself from the conversation with a promise to return when the other is calm.

***Ask your partner to tell their story.*** In any conflict, each partner has a story. Ask your partner to tell it. Listen without judgment. Try to hear their needs, feelings and values. Find something in their story to care about. Express empathy for their plight.

## 2. How to Identify Each Other's Needs

Understanding needs and feelings is the key to collaborative problem-solving. It is important to find ways to identify both your own and your partner's needs. So, take turns expressing and hearing each other's needs. Decide who will speak first. The speaker will be in "speaking mode", while the listener will be in "listening mode".

***Listening empathically.*** When the other person is in "speaking mode", your job is to listen for understanding. You want to listen carefully enough that you can repeat back what your partner is saying after they have finished speaking. You must be able to summarize what the other person has said just from listening to them.

This is difficult! In a dispute, we are usually not listening very well to the other person. We listen just long enough to plan what we want to say – usually, and attack of some sort. But in collaborative problem-solving, we want to listen empathically. We want to understand the other person's needs, feelings. We want to make the other person feel heard and understood. the best way to do this is to hear and understand the other person to his or her satisfaction.

To listen empathically:

1. Invite your partner to speak. Be curious; ask them questions. "What is your sense of what happened?" "What did you think and feeling during this event?" "What do you think you needed that you didn't receive?"

2. Put your own needs, feelings and thoughts aside. Don't defend yourself. Don't judge or criticize. For as long as your partner is speaking, put them in a box – and lock it. You'll have your opportunity to express your needs later.

3. Listen carefully to understand.

4. Don't interrupt.

5. When your partner is done speaking, summarize what they have said. Say something like, "Did I get that right?" or "Let me see if I understand what you are saying". After you summarize what they've said, ask them to correct you.

6. After your partner indicates that they feel understood, express empathy for their situation. Say something like, "If that happened to me, I'd feel angry too", or "That's an awful way to feel" or something similar.

When the other person feels heard and understood, it's time to switch roles. The speaker becomes the listener, and vice versa.

***Expressing needs.*** The best way to express needs is to use "I-statements" rather than "you-statements". "You-statements" are utterances that blame, criticize or characterize the other person (e.g., "You are always late!";

"You are responsible for losing the client", "My opponent is out-of-touch"). In contrast, I-statements describe one's own needs and feelings without blaming or criticizing the other person. An optimal "I-statement" has three parts:

1. An *observation* about something that happened.
2. A statement, using emotion words, of how one *feels*.
3. A statement of one's *needs, wants, and desires*.

There is no one way to express an I-statement. However, one effective way to express an I-statement is to word it like this:

"When you _____, I *feel* _____ because my *need* for _____ has not been met.

When we are in a dispute, understanding what our needs and feelings are is not always easy. Appendices I and II contain lists of common human needs and feelings. You'd be surprised at how helpful these lists are when you are trying to express how you feel to someone.

Here are some good I-statements:

- When you *didn't ask me about my day*, I felt *hurt* because I have a *need to be heard*.
- When you *asked me to be home before midnight*, I felt *mistrusted* because I have a *need for independence*.

- When you *told the waiter that he was too slow*, I felt *embarrassed* because I have a *need for people to be kind to each other*.
- When you *read your notes from the PowerPoint* I felt *frustrated* because I have a *need to make the audience to feel engaged*.
- When the candidate said that *she wanted to ban homeless people* from sleeping in the square, I *felt frustrated* because I have *desire to take care of the poor*.
- When the candidate said that she wanted to *allow homeless people to sleep in the square*, I felt *worried* because I have a *desire to keep the town square safe*.

Note that each of these statements (1) describes a situation without (or with a minimum of) blame or judgment, (2) explains how the person feels as a result of the situation, and (3) identifies the unmet need that led to the feelings in question. As a result, I-statements point to the self – not the other person. I-statements separate how *I* feel and what *I* want *independent* of judgments about you. They express one's own feelings and needs without blaming or making characterizations about the other person.

## 3. How to Brainstorm

If you listened carefully to each other – or even if one partner was listening very well – you will have identified the unmet needs and feelings of each party to the conflict. Now it's time to brainstorm. Both parties should work together to list as many different ways to meet the unmet needs of both parties as possible. Don't censor yourself! List all types of ideas, no matter how good, bad or unspeakable you think they are. Quite often, the bad ideas – the unspeakable ones – turn out to be the best ones. So, list, list and list. Then list some more.

## 4. How to Create Novel Solutions

Once you've listed ideas, it's time to try to create a solution to the problem of meeting the full range of unmet needs and interests expressed by the parties. You might find that some of the ideas you have generated meet some needs, but not others. You may find that some ideas meet both sets of needs at the same time. If that's true, you've solved the problem! You might find that no ideas meet the full range of needs. When that happens, you either have to generate more ideas, or work with the ones you have to modify them in ways that you meet the needs of all participants to the maximum degree possible.

Remember, most often, the best solutions are the one's no one has thought of before, or that would not be possible without both parties working together. That's because you resolve conflicts unless you know the problems that each party is trying to solve. You need the other person's perspective in order to understand the full range of the problems-to-be-solved. If you have truly identified the genuine needs of each party, solutions virtually create themselves.

## 7
## WE NEED TO CREATE CULTURES OF COLLABORATION

We are currently experiencing increasing levels of social conflict at all levels of our society. Collaborative problem solving is the key to resolving social conflict. Collaborative problem-solving is broadly applicable to managing conflict as all levels of society. It mediates the development of successful relationships, organizations, businesses and other social institutions. It can and has been used address social conflict between and among groups. It has proven effective in managing partisan[xxxiv] and other forms of political conflict – even in an increasingly polarized society.

### How to Create Cultures of Collaboration

Creating cultures of collaboration requires a transformation in our sense of selves and in our sense of who we are together. In a dispute, it is easy to see the other person as an enemy. They are stopping us from getting what we want. However, if we can see that what the other party needs deep down is not necessarily incompatible with what we need, we can turn a conflict into shared problem solving.

Let's see how it is possible to foster a culture of collaboration in different types of contexts and in relation to different types of problems. It all starts with attitude – adopting a conflict-resolution mindset as a way of live.

## Politics

Democracy consists of government by the people. The paradoxical beauty of our system of democratic government is that it seeks to use the human propensity toward competition to achieve a greater good. We live an *adversarial* democracy. Instead of resolving conflict through violence and physical confrontation, we seek to resolve conflict through debate, deliberation, political campaigns and voting. In so doing, adversarial democracy replaces *physical* confrontation with *symbolic* confrontation. Adversarial democracy works reasonably well so long as people share a set of democratic norms – a more-or-less shared common ground of beliefs and values about how democracy works (e.g., one-person-one-vote; equality of voices before the law; the transfer of power; etc.), and about what it means to be a nation.

In recent decades, democratic norms have become strained. We are losing the shared beliefs about how to engage in democratic politics. Different parties have expressed different ideas about the directions in which they want the nation to move. Against this backdrop, our adversarial democratic system has become increasingly polarized. Members of different political parties find it difficult to talk to each other. Instead of thinking of political differences as mere disagreements about how to achieve more-or-less common values, people on "the other side" are viewed as out-of-touch, stupid, crazy – and ever immoral. Debate has increasingly become a matter of "I'm right and you're evil."

Adversarial politics pits one group's position against another's. Adversarial politics creates winners and losers. The winners claim power and seek to advance their agenda. But adversarial politics is typically a zero-sum game: one party can gain only if the other party loses.

Although democracy consists of government by the people, there is nothing in democracy that says that it must be adversarial. Is it possible to create increasingly *collaborative* forms of democracy? One way to do this is to recognize that in adversarial debates, beneath each party's position in is an unmet human need. If this is so, if we focus on needs and not positions, it will often be possible to treat political issues as problems-to-be-solved collaboratively.

As a method of political conflict resolution, collaborative problem-solving seeks to find novel solutions to the problem of meeting the needs that motivate and underlie different political positions. As shown in this book, more often than we might think otherwise, while the positions that partisans take on an issue may conflict, the human needs that they are trying to meet – the problems that they are trying to solve – often do not. A collaborative approach to democracy would seek to look beyond political positioning and seek to identify the unmet human needs that people are trying to solve.

There is an enormous literature on the use of collaborative problem-solving and other forms of conflict resolution to manage and resolve political conflict on the international scene. This work shows how collaborative problem-solving has been used with various degrees of success in post-war contexts, to alleviate ethic and religious strife, in the aftermath of Apartheid, and in many other scenarios. It is perhaps ironic that collaborative problem-solving, as a form of conflict management, has not been applied to the most obvious forms of political conflict, namely everyday partisan politics and the problem of political polarization.

Research in our group has shown that people from different political orientations can indeed use collaborative problem-solving to create shared solutions to difficult political problems.[xxxiv] We taught a group of people from different political orientations the principles and practices of collaborative problem-solving. Over a series of months, the author moderated the group as they engaged in a series of discussions directed toward proposing solutions to a series of contentious political conflicts. These conflicts included minor issues like whether schools should require uniforms, as well as major ones related to capital punishment and race relations involving police. Over a series of months, the group was able to achieve massive levels of consensus on how to resolve deeply contentious social problems. The study showed that it is possible for people who hold different political views to bridge political divides on seemingly intractable social issues.

It is thus possible to create collaborative forms of political problem-solving that bridge political divides. The question becomes how this can be done on a larger scale – that is, how we can usher in cultures of collaboration to address social issues at increasingly broad levels of political engagement. One way to answer this question is to invoke a useful maxim: "think globally, act locally". Instead of trying to produce sweeping changes in the structure of democratic processes at the national level, it is better to try to change the process of problem-solving in local spheres of action – at the level of municipalities, neighborhoods, local meetings, and other venues in which people confront social problems[1].

---

[1] To introduce a collaborative culture within local levels, to solve any given local problem, it is first necessary to seek to identify the *genuine* needs, interests, concerns and grievances of all stakeholders. This is a nuanced process. Although people tend to be good at articulating their positions on an issue, they are less skilled at identifying their deeper needs. For example, asked to identify one's unmet needs regarding the social problem of homelessness, a person might say, "I want the homeless off of the main square." Another might say, "We should build expand rooms at the homeless shelter." Both statements are expressions of *positions* – not needs. These are preferred *solutions* to the problem at hand. What are the deeper unmet needs or problems that motivate such positions? A need would be more like, "I have

Leaders who become well-versed in collaborative problem-solving can produce shared solutions that will ultimately demonstrate its effectiveness. Collaborative political discourse can then ripple through communities, cities, states and beyond to provide genuine alternatives to adversarial forms of democracy.

## Organizations and Businesses

Businesses and organizations tend to be hierarchical enterprises. Owners and CEOs direct supervisors, who thereupon direct increasingly lower levels of subordinates. In a typical organizational culture, people higher in the hierarchy tend to enjoy authority. Because employees at the lower tiers of an organization work at the discretion of their bosses, authority tends to foster fear. As a result, employees are typically reluctant to voice their ideas or concerns out of fear of reprisal. Nonetheless, employees will necessarily have needs, concerns and grievances, and will often have useful and important insights about how to improve an organization's operations. When employees fail to give voice to their needs and ideas, they suffer. But they are

---

a need for a *safe and crime-free* downtown" or "I am trying to solve the problem of finding *housing* for the homeless". These statements are open-ended problems. As such, people can work together to solve them in different ways. For example, there are many ways of keeping the downtown safe and crime-free other than banning the homeless; there are many ways of housing the homeless other than expanding a shelter. What solutions meet both sets of needs?

not the only ones. Employers also suffer because they never become aware of issues, needs and problems that are essential for them to fulfill their missions.

There is thus a need for collaboration within organizations and businesses. Collaboration is necessary between employees and employers, between the organization and its clients, between the organization and the full range of its stakeholders. Considering this goal, it is tempting to seek to replace a hierarchically structured organization with a collaborative one. There are indeed many examples of successful organizations that have adopted collaborative structures between and among employers and employees. These include cooperatives; employee-owned businesses, deliberately developmental organizations, and so forth.

Such structures, however, tend to be difficult to develop and maintain. This is because there are inescapable and even necessary inequalities in any organization. Inequalities and status differences arise as a function of ownership, degree of responsibility, knowledge, skill, and other variables. An entrepreneur who has worked long and hard to develop a business and a vision may indeed be entitled to greater authority over employees. An individual with less expertise in business processes may not be able to contribute to the betterment of an organization as much as more expert people. A degree of hierarchization is typically required.

Organizations and business need some way of coordinating hierarchy and collaboration to thrive. To reach such a reproachment, CEO's, bosses and supervisors must realize that they cannot know everything. To be sure, there is a need for leaders to be directive. However, a good leader is one who can mobilize people in the direction of a shared goal. And so, a good leader must also be open, sensitive and collaborative. As one example of how this can be done, consider the case of an interim President of a university. In many colleges, faculty and administration engage in a form of leadership that is called *shared governance:* faculty are responsible for overseeing academic matters, while administrations are charged managing finances and infrastructure. As a broad unit, the faculties tend to organize itself as a kind of democracy. Faculty members vote on important educational issues and programs. On the other hand, administrations tend to be organized as more traditional corporate hierarchies. The result is that presidents are charged with the task of sharing leadership in an organization composed of a various units – some hierarchical, others more autonomous.

The model often fails to work well. Faculty and administration often fight fiercely over core issues. Different factions within the university tend to compete for limited resources. Leaders of each division are praised for the extent to which they can "advocate" for their divisions – to get as much of the limited pie of resources as possible. The result is a zero-sum game in which resources allocated to any one division come at the expense of those solicited by others.

One interim President sought to solve this problem in a collaborative way. He changed the organizational structure of the administration from a largely hierarchical one into a kind of "collaborative hierarchy". He brought the heads of various divisions in the college -- both faculty and the administrative -- together into a single body that he called the "supercommittee". The supercommittee was charged with collective decision-making for the entire university. In this body, each division was able to articulate their needs and problems to all other members of the committee. Because problems of each division were solved collaboratively, *each member of the committee was aware of the needs and problems that each other member of the committee was trying to address and had to take those needs into consideration when deliberating any issue.* Each constituency faced the task of having to play a role in coordinating their needs with the needs of other divisions and with the university as a whole. Under such circumstances, it became difficult for any single constituency to advocate for themselves at the expense of others. The group was able to understand the interrelatedness of each other's needs and problems, a situation that fostered relationships, trust, collaborative problem-solving and novel ways of resolving problems.

Another example of a collaborative organization involves a supermarket chain in Massachusetts (USA) called *Market Basket.* Market Basket is a business owned by the Demoulas family. The owners sought to organize the company explicitly around as if it were a kind of family. The mantra of the company was "people first, profits second." Toward this end, the supermarket chain engaged in the practice of opening supermarkets in poorer communities, hiring people from those communities, training employees in all aspects of the supermarket so that they could rise professionally in the company, keeping prices low, and ensuring that well-trained workers were visibly available for customers during store hours. This produced a strong sense of loyalty among both employees and customers.

In 2014, one of the brothers, Arthur T. Demoulas orchestrated a take-over of the supermarket chain from his brother Arthur S. Demoulas. The attempted takeover resulted in a strike on the part of the employees across the entire corporation. The employees protested Arthur's T.'s intention to transform the business from its "family orientation" to a more corporate and hierarchical approach. The strike was supported not only by the workers, but also by the customers, who elected to shop at more expensive stores over the course of the strike. The strike was remarkably successful, and *Market Basket* continues to operate in a people-oriented and collaborative fashion.

## Children, Parents and Schools

If we are to have a chance to usher in cultures of collaboration, it is generally best to begin at the beginning -- with children. We will be most able to create cultures of collaboration if we teach children how to become collaborative beings. This means teaching them to resolve conflict with others through *collaboration* and problem-solving rather than through opposition. It means cultivating moral character by teaching *relational values to live by* – values like compassion, care, humility, and responsibility. It is possible to do this both in homes and in schools. Doing so calls on us to make subtle shifts in how we think about how we deal with conflict both at home and in schools.

Sometimes, people will look at two children fighting over a toy and say, "Don't intervene – let them work it out!" The fear is that the parent or educator will solve the problem for the children and thereupon rob the children of the opportunity to learn to solve the problem themselves. But this is not true. There is a difference between solving problems *for oneself* and solving problems *by oneself*. Hundreds of studies in developmental psychology show that *learning occurs through doing*. To learn something, we must actively engage in the activity we want to learn! One doesn't learn tennis by being told how to play. One needs to be coached as one is playing the game. And so, to learn a new skill, we must learn desired activities *for ourselves* -- but not necessarily *by ourselves*.

This is especially true when teaching children how to resolve social problems collaboratively. If adults do a poor job resolving conflict together, why would we expect children to do better? If we want children to learn to resolve conflicts, we should neither let them work it out themselves nor should we resolve the problem for them. Instead, we should show children how to resolve conflict and guide them through the process of resolving conflict with the other person. Over time, they will learn to do it by themselves and without assistance.

But there's more. Creating a culture of conflict resolution in homes and schools requires more than simply teaching children how to resolve conflict. It requires that we – as teachers, educators and leaders – adopt a collaborative approach to family and school life! We should engage each other in collaborative problem-solving and conflict resolution as a matter of course. When we do so, we model the process for children. When we engage children in the process collaborative problem-solving, they become guided participants in the process. Guided participation in skilled activities is the most powerful form of learning.

It is important to note that embracing collaborative problem-solving as a way of life *does not require parents or teachers to relinquish one iota of their legitimate authority*. It is sometimes thought that when we collaborate, we give up power or authority. This is simply not true. To the extent that that parents and teachers know more and are responsible for a child's wellbeing, parents and teachers have legitimate authority over that child. Optimally, when a parent or teacher engages in collaborative problem-solving with a child, they should do as a deliberate choice – because they think that the process will contribute to the development and well-being of the child. Doing so is a way of *exercising* authority – not relinquishing it.

And further, as indicated above, conflict management is not *kumbaya*. It involves seeking solutions to problems *without giving in* on one's core needs. Parents and teachers should not "give in" on their core goals and concerns for their children. Imagine a parent or teacher is trying to get a child to complete a homework assignment. You might think, "Engage in collaborative problem-solving with a child over the issue of homework? Are you crazy?" It would indeed be crazy to collaborate over *whether* the child is to do the homework. But this is not going to happen – because the parent's inviolate need is to have the child complete the homework!

Collaboration is not about positions (e.g., arguing over whether to do homework); it's about *how to meet needs and solve problems*. The parent's or teacher's need is for the child to do the homework. That is inviolate. However, if the child is avoiding homework, we must find out why. What is the child's need, problem or difficulty? Imagine that the child avoids the homework because of its difficulty or unpleasantness. Taking that problem into account, the parent and child may indeed be able to engage in collaborative-problem solving about *how* to approach the homework. This will be done with the parent fully "in charge". The question becomes: "How can we find a way for the child to simultaneously complete the homework while also dealing with the problem of difficulty?" There are many solutions to this problem: help the child; get a tutor; encourage the child to take breaks; break down the task for the child, etc.

Another obstacle to creating cultures of collaboration in the home is the idea that the parents need to create "a united front" in relation to the children. Parents may feel that they must first agree on how to address a problem with their children before implementing a solution. But this is not necessarily so. Because collaborative problem-solving is about meeting the needs of people in conflict, it is not necessary for parents to "agree" on a solution beforehand. All they need to do is to be committed to finding ways to meet each other's (and the child's) needs. Parents can engage in collaborative problem-solving in public or in private – but doing so in front of the children (and even with children) doesn't harm the children. Instead, it models and teaches the process itself! Children learn to resolve conflict when they see the caring and respectful process of collaboration modelled in front of them as part of the everyday culture of the home. The parents don't need a "united front" because they are seeking to create a solution to a problem *that unites everyone* – without giving in or necessarily making compromises.

If we want collaborative cultures, we should implement cultures of collaboration in the home and the school. Schools are an ideal venue for teaching conflict resolution and collaborative problem-solving – from an early age onward. We should proactively teach children how to manage conflict and actively use conflict management to mediate and resolve conflicts between and among children, teachers, and parents. The best way to foster cultures of collaboration among adults is to foster the development of collaborative skills in children.

## Creating Cultures of Collaboration

*Do I not destroy my enemies when I make them my friends?*

-- Abraham Lincoln

In a dispute, the moment we realize that the other party's actions are motivated by some unmet need, we have humanized them. We begin to cease thinking of the other as an obstacle or an enemy. We can now think of them as a person who is trying to solve a problem. We can begin to see that if we want to solve our problem, we can do so by helping the other solve theirs. And when we see this, we begin to see how, even as individuals, we rely on each other – even our "enemies" – in our everyday lives.

To create cultures of collaboration, we first must how to resolve conflict, solve problems, and develop our relationships with others. Once we gain some proficiency in doing this, we can bring our newfound skills into our local spheres of influence. Those areas could include our relationships, families, schools, houses of worship, workplaces, and municipalities.

The more we do this, the more we will find that the cultures in which we operate will also change (even if only a little). Small changes beget larger changes; and larger changes ripple outward into communities. This is how we change our worlds – slowly and gradually – thinking globally but acting locally.

## APPENDIX I: A LIST OF HUMAN NEEDS

Here are some words that refer to human needs. (This list is an extended adaptation from the *Needs Inventory* provided by the *Center for Non-Violent Communication*.)

**Autonomy**
Choice
Freedom
Independence
Initiative
Power
Spontaneity

**Connection**
Acceptance
Affection
Appreciation
Belonging
Cooperation
Communication
Closeness
Community
Companionship
Compassion
Consideration
Consistency
Emotional Safety
Empathy
Intimacy
Kindness
Love
Mutuality
Nurturing
Respect
Partnership
Security
Stability
Support
Transparency

**Connection (continued)**
To Know
To Be Known
To Be Seen
To Understand
To Be Understood
Trust
Warmth

**Community**
Cooperation
Equality
Fellowship
Inclusion
Interdependence
Harmony
Justice
Mutuality
Participation
Reciprocity
Solidarity

**Honesty**
Authenticity
Integrity
Presence

**Meaning**
Awareness
Celebration of Life
Challenge
Clarity

**Meaning (continued)**
Competence
Consciousness
Contribution
Creativity
Discovery
Efficacy
Effectiveness
Growth
Hope
Inspiration
Learning
Mourning
Participation
Purpose
Self-Expression
Simplicity
Stimulation
To Matter
Understanding

**Peace**
Appreciation
Balance
Beauty
Communion
Equanimity
Ease
Gratitude
Order
Predictability
Tranquility

# APPENDIX II: A LIST OF HUMAN EMOTIONS

Here are some words that refer to human feelings. (This list is an extended adaptation from the *Feelings Inventory* provided by the *Center for Non-Violent Communication*.)

## *Words that Name Feelings When Needs are Met*

**Affectionate**
Caring
Compassionate
Friendly
Loving
Open-hearted
Sympathetic
Tender
Warm

**Engaged**
Absorbed
Alert
Curious
Engrossed
Enchanted
Entranced
Fascinated
Interested
Intrigued
Involved
Spellbound
Stimulated

**Exhilarated**
Blissful
Ecstatic
Elated
Enthralled
Exuberant
Radiant
Rapturous
Thrilled

**Hopeful**
Expectant
Encouraged
Optimistic

**Confident**
Empowered
Open
Proud
Safe
Secure

**Excited**
Amazed
Animated
Ardent
Aroused
Astonished
Dazzled
Eager
Energetic
Enthusiastic
Giddy
Invigorated
Lively
Passionate
Playful
Surprised
Vibrant

**Grateful**
Appreciative
Blessed
Fortunate
Humble
Lucky
Moved
Thankful
Touched

**Inspired**
Adventurous
Amazed
Awed
Wonder

**Joyful**
Amused
Delighted
Glad
Happy
Jubilant
Pleased
Tickled

**Peaceful**
Calm
Clear Headed
Comfortable
Centered
Content
Equanimous
Fulfilled

## *Words that Name Feelings When Needs are Unmet*

**Annoyed**
Aggravated
Cynical
Dismayed
Disgruntled
Displeased
Exasperated
Frustrated
Impatient
Irritated
Irked

**Angry**
Bitter
Disdain
Enraged
Furious
Incensed
Irate
Livid
Outraged
Resentful
Resistant
Vindictive

**Aversion**
Animosity
Appalled
Contempt
Disgusted
Dislike
Hate
Horrified
Hostile
Repulsed

**Confused**
Ambivalent
Baffled
Bewildered
Dazed
Lost
Mystified
Perplexed
Puzzled
Torn

**Disconnected**
Alienated
Aloof
Apathetic
Bored
Cold
Detached
Distant
Distracted
Empty
Hurt
Indifferent
Isolated
Lonely
Numb
Removed
Uninterested
Withdrawn

**Disquiet**
Agitated
Disconcerted
Disturbed
Moody
Perturbed
Surprised
Trouble

**Disquieted
(continued)**
Uncomfortable
Uneasy
Unsettled
Upset

**Embarrassed**
Ashamed
Humiliated
Inhibited
Mortified
Self-Conscious
Useless
Unworthy

**Fatigue**
Beat
Burnt Out
Depleted
Exhausted
Lethargic
Listless
Sleepy
Tired
Weary
Worn Out

**Fear**
Alarmed
Afraid
Apprehensive
Hesitant
Panic
Shocked
Startled
Terrified
Unsafe
Worried

**Guilt**
Chagrined
Chastened
Contrite
Regretful
Remorseful
Sorry

**Pain**
Agony
Anguished
Devastated
Miserable

**Powerless**
Impotent
Incapable
Resigned
Trapped
Victimized

**Sadness**
Bereaved
Depressed
Dejected
Despair
Despondent
Disappointed
Discouraged
Disheartened
Forlorn
Gloomy
Grief
Heartbroken
Hopeless
Melancholy
Shut Down
Sorrow
Unhappy

# Notes

i Druckman J. N., Klar, S. et al., (2024). *Partisan Hostility and American Democracy: Explaining Political Divisions and When They Matter.* Chicago University Press

ii Artman, R., Hester, N., & Gray, K. (2023). People see political opponents as more stupid than evil. *Personality and Social Psychology Bulletin*, 49, 1014–1027, doi: 10.1177/01461672221089451.

iii Mordocco, E., & Buonvino, C. C. (2019). Dealing with conflicts within organisations. In *Gestalt approaches with organisations*. (pp. 245–261). Istituto di Gestalt HCC Italy.

iv Eisenbraun, K. D. (2007). Violence in schools: Prevalence, prediction, and prevention. *Aggression and Violent Behavior*, *12*(4), 459–469. https://doi-org.proxy3.noblenet.org/10.1016/j.avb.2006.09.008; Ogg, J., Anthony, C. J., & Wendel, M. (2024). Student-teacher conflict or student-school conflict? Exploring bidirectional relationships between externalizing behavior and teacher conflict. *Early Childhood Research Quarterly*, *67*, 44–54. https://doi-org.proxy3.noblenet.org/10.1016/j.ecresq.2023.11.002

v Sommer, F., Leuschner, V., & Scheithauer, H. (2014). Bullying, romantic rejection, and conflicts with teachers: The crucial role of social dynamics in the development of school shootings—A systematic review. *International Journal of Developmental Science*, *8*(1–2), 3–24.

vi Birditt, K.S., Brown, E., Orbuch, T.L., & McIlvane, J. M. (2010). Marital conflict behaviors and implications for divorce over 16 Years. *Journal of Marriage and Family*, 72, 1188-1204. doi: 10.1111/j.1741-3737.2010.00758.x.; Martínez-Pampliega, A., Cormenzana, S., Corral, S., Iraurgi, I., Iraurgi, I., & Sanz, M. (2021). Family structure, interparental conflict & adolescent symptomatology. *Journal of Family Studies*, *27*(2), 231–246. https://doi-org.proxy3.noblenet.org/10.1080/13229400.2018.1536609

[vii] Kelman, H., C. (1996). Negotiation as interactive problem solving. *International Negotiation: A Journal of Theory and Practice*, 1, 99-123

[viii] Kelman, H., C. (1999) Transforming the relationship between former enemies: A social-psychological analysis. In: In R.L. Rothstein (Ed.), *After the peace: Resistance and reconciliation* (pp. 193-205). Lynne Rienner.

[ix] Kelman, H.C. (2010). Interactive problem solving: Changing political cultural in the pursuit of conflict resolution *Peace and Conflict: Journal of Peace Psychology*, 16, 389-413.

[x] Novaes, C. D. (2023). Can arguments change minds? Proceedings of the Aristotelian Society, 123, 173-198, https://doi.org/10.1093/arisoc/aoad006

[xi] Fisher, R., Ury, W. L., & Patton, B. (2011). *Getting to yes: Negotiating agreement without giving in* (3rd Edition). Penguin Books

[xii] Fülöp, M. (2009). Happy and unhappy competitors: What makes the difference? *Psihologijske Teme*, *18*, 345–367; Dumitriu, D. L. (2013). Framing sports failure: Shame as a climax of disappointment. In *The walk of shame.* (pp. 211–233). Nova Science Publishers; Weiss, K. N., Hameiri, B., & Halperin, E. (2020). Group-based guilt and shame in the context of intergroup conflict: The role of beliefs and meta-beliefs about group malleability. *Journal of Applied Social Psychology*, *50*, 213–227. https://doi-org.proxy3.noblenet.org/10.1111/jasp.12651

[xiii] Mascolo, M. F. (2021). *From conflict to collaboration: A step-by-step process to solving problems in everyday relationships.* Absolute Author.

[xiv] Fisher, R., Ury, W. L., & Patton, B. (2011). *Getting to yes: Negotiating agreement without giving in* (3rd Edition). Penguin Books

[xv] Mascolo, M. F. Bridging partisan divides: Dialectical engagement and deep sociality. *Journal of Constructivist Psychology, 35*, 877–903, 2022. Doi: 10.1080/10720537.2020.1805065; Sasaki, E., & Overall, N. C. (2023). Constructive conflict resolution requires tailored responsiveness to specific needs. *Current Opinion in Psychology, 52.* https://doi-org.proxy3.noblenet.org/10.1016/j.copsyc.2023.101638;

Shnabel, N, & Nadler, A. (2008). A needs-based model of reconciliation: Satisfying the differential emotional needs of victim and perpetrator as a key to promoting reconciliation. *Journal of Personality and Social Psychology* 94, 116–312. doi:10.1037/0022-3514.94.1.116.

xvi Fisher, R., Ury, W. L., & Patton, B. (2011). *Getting to yes: Negotiating agreement without giving in* (3rd Edition). Penguin Books

xvii Rigdon, M., Clark, C., & Hershgold, E. (1993). A case demonstration of two methods for promoting the credulous approach in personal construct psychotherapy. In *Critical issues in personal construct psychotherapy.* (pp. 157–172). Robert E Krieger Publishing Co.

xviii Kappmeier, M. (2016). Trusting the enemy—Towards a comprehensive understanding of trust in intergroup conflict. *Peace and Conflict: Journal of Peace Psychology, 22*, 134–144. https://doi-org.proxy3.noblenet.org/10.1037/pac0000159; Klimecki, O. M. (2019). The role of empathy and compassion in conflict resolution. *Emotion Review, 11*, 310–325. https://doi-org.proxy3.noblenet.org/10.1177/1754073919838609

xix Lindner, E. G. (2009). Why there can be no conflict resolution as long as people are being humiliated. *International Review of Education, 55*(2/3), 157–181. https://doi-org.proxy3.noblenet.org/10.1007/s11159-008-9125-9; Murithi, T. (2009). An African perspective on peace education: Ubuntu lessons in reconciliation, *International Review of Education, 55*, 221–233. https://doi-org.proxy3.noblenet.org/10.1007/s11159-009-9129-0

xx Macmurray, J. (1962/1998). *Persons in relation.* Humanities Press.

xxi Dupre, John. (2002) *Human nature and the limits of science:* Oxford University Press; Zafirovaski, M. (2003). The rational choice approach to human studies: A reexamination. *Human Studies, 26*, 41. https://doi-org.proxy3.noblenet.org/10.1023/A:1022531732652;

xxii Knafo, A., Zahn-Waxler, C., Van Hulle, C., Robinson, J. L., & Rhee, S. H. (2008). The developmental origins of a disposition toward empathy: Genetic and environmental contributions. *Emotion*, *8*(6), 737–752. https://doi-org.proxy3.noblenet.org/10.1037/a0014179

[xxiii] Frimer, J. A., & Walker, L. J. (2009). Reconciling the self and morality: An empirical model of moral centrality development. *Developmental Psychology*, *45*(6), 1669–1681. https://doi-org.proxy3.noblenet.org/10.1037/a0017418

[xxiv] Paulus, M., Becher, T., Christner, N., Kammermeier, M., Gniewosz, B., & Pletti, C. (2024). When do children begin to care for others? The ontogenetic growth of empathic concern across the first two years of life. *Cognitive Development*, *70*, N.PAG. https://doi-org.proxy3.noblenet.org/10.1016/j.cogdev.2024.101439

[xxv] Davidov, M., Paz, Y., Roth-Hanania, R., Uzefovsky, F., Orlitsky, T., Mankuta, D., & Zahn-Waxler, C. (2021). Caring babies: Concern for others in distress during infancy. *Developmental Science*, *24*(2). https://doi-org.proxy3.noblenet.org/10.1111/desc.13016

[xxvi] Paz, Y., Davidov, M., Orlitsky, T., Roth, H. R., & Zahn, W. C. (2022). Developmental trajectories of empathic concern in infancy and their links to social competence in early childhood. *Journal of Child Psychology*, *63*, 762–770. https://doi-org.proxy3.noblenet.org/10.1111/jcpp.13516

[xxvii] Dahl, A. (2020). Early developments in acts and evaluations of helping: When and how to help? In L. A. Jensen (Ed.), *The Oxford handbook of moral development: An interdisciplinary perspective.* (pp. 288–305). Oxford University Press; Dahl, A. (2015). The developing social context of infant helping in two U.S. samples. *Child Development*, *86*, 1080–1093. https://doi-org.proxy3.noblenet.org/10.1111/cdev.12361

[xxviii] Feldman, R. (2007). Mother-infant synchrony and the development of moral orientation in childhood and adolescence: Direct and indirect mechanisms of developmental continuity. *American Journal of Orthopsychiatry*, *77*, 582–597. https://doi-org.proxy3.noblenet.org/10.1037/0002-9432.77.4.582

[xxix] Fow, N. R. (2003). The call to caring. *The Humanistic Psychologist*, *31*(1), 22–42. https://doi-org.proxy3.noblenet.org/10.1080/08873267.2003.9986918; Garrido-Macías, M., Navarro-Carrillo, G., Soler-Martínez,

F. M., & Valor-Segura, I. (2023). Disentangling the road to a compassionate response to suffering: A multistudy investigation. *Personality & Individual Differences, 203*, https://doi-org.proxy3.noblenet.org/10.1016/j.paid.2022.112030

[xxx] Chigangaidze, R. K., & Chinyenze, P. (2022). What it means to say, *'a person is a person through other persons'*: Ubuntu through humanistic-existential lenses of transactional analysis. *Journal of Religion & Spirituality in Social Work: Social Thought, 41*(3), 280–295. https://doi-org.proxy3.noblenet.org/10.1080/15426432.2022.2039341

[xxxi] *Fromm, E. (1956). The art of loving.* HarperPerennial.

[xxxii] Kelman, H., C. (2004). Reconciliation as identity change: A social psychological perspective. In: In Y. Bar-Siman-Tov (Ed.) *From conflict resolution to reconciliation* (pp. 111-124); Oxford; Waghid, Y., & Smeyers, P. (2012). Reconsidering "Ubuntu": On the educational potential of a particular ethic of care. *Educational Philosophy and Theory, 44*, 6–20.

[xxxiii] Hanks, T. L. (2008). The Ubuntu paradigm: Psychology's next force? *Journal of Humanistic Psychology, 48*(1), 116–135; Mogadime, D., Mentz, P. J., Armstrong, D. E., & Holtam, B. (2010). Constructing self as leader: Case studies of women who are change agents in South Africa. *Urban Education, 45*, 797–821. https://doi-org.proxy3.noblenet.org/10.1177/0042085910384203

[xxxiv] Mascolo, M. F. (2024). Toward a more collaborative democracy: Bridging political divides through dialectical problem-solving. In Shannon, N., Mascolo, M. F., & Belolutskaya, A. (Eds.). *Routledge International Handbook of Dialectical Thinking.* Routledge.; Mascolo, M. F. (2022). Bridging partisan divides: Dialectical engagement and deep sociality. *Journal of Constructivist Psychology*, 35, 877–903. . Doi: 10.1080/10720537.2020.1805065; Pilisuk, M. (1997). Resolving Ideological Clashes Through Dialogue: Abortion as a Case Study. *Peace & Conflict, 3*(2), 135.

# ABOUT THE AUTHOR

Michael F. Mascolo, Ph.D. is Director of Creating Common Ground, Inc (www.creatingcommonground.org), a nonprofit whose mission is to help people bridge divides of contentious interpersonal, social and political issues. He is Professor of Psychology (Emeritus) at Merrimack College in North Andover, Massachusetts. He is the author, editor or co-editor of seven books, including most *The Routledge International Handbook of Dialectical Thinking* (2024, with Nicholas Shannon & Anastasia Belolutskya, Routledge), *From Conflict to Collaboration: A Step-by-Step Approach to Solving Problems in Everyday Relationships* (2021, Absolute Author), *The Handbook of Integrative Developmental Science* (with Thomas Bidell, 2020, Routledge) *8 Keys to Old School Parenting for Modern Day Families* (2015, Norton), *Psychotherapy as a Developmental Process* (2010, with Michael Basseches, Routledge, Taylor & Francis), *Culture and Self* (with Jin Li, 2004, Jossey-Bass), and *What Develops in Emotional Development* (1998, with Sharon Griffin, Plenum). He is also author of over 100 scholarly articles on issues related to human development and is a regular contributor to *Creating Common Ground* Online Magazine. He can be reached at michaelmascolo@creatingcommonground.org.

Made in the USA
Columbia, SC
07 November 2024

45345942R00050